W9-CLU-665

DISCARD

ANCIENT EGYPT

DISCARD

Ancient Egypt

DISCARD

CHARLES ALEXANDER ROBINSON, JR.
REVISED BY LORNA GREENBERG

A First Book | Revised Edition
FRANKLIN WATTS | 1984
New York | London | Toronto | Sydney

1/85 STS 8⁹⁰

J
932
R

47633

FRONTIS: THE HYPOSTYLE HALL OF THE
TEMPLE OF AMUN AT KARNAK

Map by Vantage Art, Inc.

Cover photograph courtesy of
The Metropolitan Musem of Art (substantially restored)

Photographs courtesy of: Hugo Vandenwallbake: frontispiece, pp. 13, 32;
Robert B. Strassler: pp. 2, 45, 53, 57; The Metropolitan Museum of Art:
pp. 7 (Dodge Fund, 1931), 8 (Rogers Fund, 1911), 16 (Rogers Fund, 1915),
19 (Museum Excavations, 1919-1920, supplemented by contributions from
Edward S. Harkness and Rogers Fund, 1920), 27 (Gift of Mrs. Myron C.
Taylor, 1938), 28 (Museum Excavations, 1922-1923, Rogers Fund, 1923),
37, 38 (Egyptian Expedition), 42 (Rogers Fund, 1908), 46 (Museum
Excavations, 1928-1929 and Rogers Fund, 1930), 24, 25, 34, 50.

Library of Congress Cataloging in Publication Data

Robinson, Charles Alexander, 1900-1965.
Ancient Egypt.

(A First book)
Bibliography: p.
Includes index.
Summary: Traces the history of ancient Egypt through
the dynasties, describing daily life, farming and trade,
religion, architecture, literature, and science.
1. Egypt—Civilization—To 332 B.C.—Juvenile litera-
ture. [1. Egypt—History—To 332 B.C. 2. Egypt—
Civilization—To 332 B.C.] I. Greenberg, Lorna. II. Title.
DT61.R53   1984   932'.01   84-3653
ISBN 0-531-04819-5

Second Edition
Copyright © 1961, 1984 by Franklin Watts, Inc.
All rights reserved
Printed in the United States of America
6   5   4   3   2   1

CONTENTS

FOR MY GRANDCHILDREN

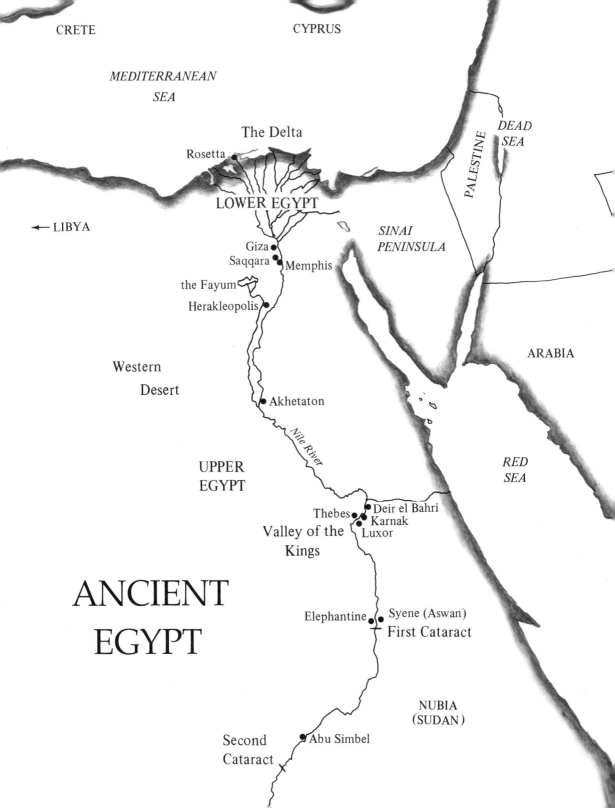

CRETE

CYPRUS

MEDITERRANEAN SEA

The Delta

Rosetta

DEAD SEA

LOWER EGYPT

PALESTINE

← LIBYA

SINAI PENINSULA

Giza
Saqqara
Memphis

the Fayum

Herakleopolis

ARABIA

Western Desert

Akhetaton

Nile River

UPPER EGYPT

RED SEA

Thebes
Valley of the Kings
Deir el Bahri
Karnak
Luxor

ANCIENT EGYPT

Elephantine
Syene (Aswan)
First Cataract

NUBIA (SUDAN)

Second Cataract

Abu Simbel

EGYPT AND THE NILE

In a very real sense, Egypt and the River Nile are one. If it had not been for the Nile, all Egypt would have been a desert. The great civilization that grew up along its banks five thousand years ago would never have been born.

The Nile is formed by two great streams: the Blue Nile which rises in the highlands of Ethiopia; and the White Nile, from the lake regions of East Africa. They join at Khartoum in the Sudan, and from there run north to the Mediterranean. Along this course, in ancient times, the life-giving river forced the bitter desert to yield one long strip of fertile land.

At six points between Khartoum and the sea, the river passes through rapids, called the Nile Cataracts. The Sixth Cataract is near Khartoum. The numbers are counted down as the river flows north to the sea. The First Cataract is at Aswan, and this marks the Nile's entry into the land of ancient Egypt. Today at Aswan (the ancient Syene) there is a modern high dam that controls the Nile's floodwaters and provides electric power.

From Aswan the Nile continues 600 miles (965 km) to Cairo, where the ancient city of Memphis stood. Through this whole distance the river flows between limestone hills in a valley only 10 to 30 miles (16 to 48 km) wide. In ancient times this area, from Syene almost as far as Memphis, was called Upper Egypt.

At Cairo the hills disappear, and the Nile flows for over 100 miles (161 km) through flat and marshy land to empty, by several channels, into the Mediterranean Sea. This part of the country

**The Nile was the source of life for the land of
ancient Egypt—as well as its great highway.**

was Lower Egypt. It is often called the Delta because its triangular shape resembles the fourth letter of the Greek alphabet.

The 4,132-mile (6,648-km) long Nile is the longest river in the world. But the most remarkable thing about the Nile was that every summer the monsoons, or tropical rains, in Ethiopia caused it to rise and overflow its banks and flood the land. Everything beyond the reach of the overflow was desert, but as the water returned to its channel in December, it left a rich deposit of earth, or silt, on the land it had covered. This soil was fertile and so dark in color that the ancient Egyptians called their land *kemet*, the "black land," to distinguish it from the barren desert surrounding it—the "red land."

Here, in the valley of the Nile, the splendid Egyptian civilization began. The lands along the Nile were rich enough to be farmed, and the crops could feed a settled people—once the ancient Egyptians found ways to store the yearly floodwaters and then use them for irrigating during the dry, growing season. The farmers learned to lift water out of the Nile or out of wells and send it across the fields through a system of canals. To do this, the people had to work together; no one person could do it alone. As scattered farmers and villages began to cooperate, a structure or organization started to grow. Leaders emerged to direct and plan the work. A form of government developed. When people live and work together in groups, under a central government, they soon begin to build cities, to manufacture things, to trade with their neighbors. A civilization emerges. This is what happened in Egypt.

By 3100 B.C., the Egyptians created a central government and lived in cities. They used metals and a form of writing. They still shaped their pottery by hand, but were soon to learn to work the clay on a crude, horizontal wheel—actually a turntable. This was a potter's wheel and it enabled the people to make their bowls more quickly and to develop skills to create beautiful objects.

Once the Egyptians learned to work metals—particularly how to mix tin and copper to make bronze—they were able to make better tools than the stone ones they had used earlier. But what was even more important, this new knowledge stirred their imaginations. One invention led to another.

As trade and government grew, the Egyptians needed a way to keep records. By about 3100 B.C. they were using a form of picture writing that the Greeks later named hieroglyphics, or sacred carvings, because they first saw them on Egyptian temple walls. Pictures and symbols were carved on stone or painted with reed pens and brushes dipped in red and black ink made of gum and colored earth. A simpler, cursive (flowing) form of writing, called hieratic (priestly), evolved from hieroglyphics. It was quicker to write and was used for ordinary documents. Later an even simpler form, demotic (of the people), developed.

The writing material the Egyptians invented was used throughout most of the ancient world. It was made by pressing together flat strips cut from the stalks of the papyrus plant that grew in the marshes along the Nile. Since these strips were usually long, the Egyptians rolled their writing paper into cylinders when they were not using it.

There were other areas in which Egyptian ideas and inventions led in new, creative directions. The beginnings of medical science and geometry, the creation of a 365-day calendar, a monumental and splendid architecture, an expressive style of art, and an appreciation of beauty, are all part of the Egyptian civilization.

So too was a strong religion that shaped every part of Egyptian life. Because the religion stressed a life after death, the Egyptians stored away treasures and supplies for their next life. They built tombs, and prepared papyri with records and pictures of their lives. From all these preserved riches, prepared for a life after that on earth, we can learn about the Egyptians' actual life in this world.

EARLY EGYPT AND THE OLD KINGDOM

The earliest traces of human life in the Nile region are from the Paleolithic Age (Old Stone Age), about 300,000 B.C., at the very edges of the Nile Valley. Early people of this time had no permanent dwellings; they moved from place to place, eating berries, roots, and any animal life they could find. During the Neolithic Age (New Stone Age), about 6000 to 4300 B.C., they slowly began to make stone tools, to grow crops, and herd animals. At about this time, changes in the world climate and geography brought small groups of other peoples into the Nile Valley—from the Upper Nile Region, from Asia Minor, and perhaps from North Africa. Over the following centuries, these different groups mingled to form the ancestors of the Egyptian people. By about 4000 B.C., the people lived in huts of mud bricks or mud and reeds. They kept livestock, they farmed, fished, and hunted, they traded and made pottery and flint tools and jewelry. They buried their dead in shallow graves, along with objects of daily use.

In time, the small settlements gradually combined into larger units until two kingdoms evolved: the Kingdom of Upper Egypt, which was the region south of the Nile delta, along the two banks of the river; and the kingdom of Lower Egypt, the delta itself.

The date 3100 B.C., in two important ways, marks the beginning of the history of Egypt. It was about this time that a system of writing began to be used in the Nile region. Earlier times are called "prehistoric," and the history of Egypt begins at this point.

It was at about 3100 B.C. that Egypt as a state was created: the two kingdoms, Upper Egypt and Lower Egypt, were united, to form the one nation of Egypt.

The story of how Egypt became one state is shown in ancient paintings and carvings, but it is difficult to separate history from the legends that surround it. We believe that about 3100 B.C. mighty King Narmer of Upper Egypt conquered Lower Egypt and became ruler of the united kingdom. From this time, the king often wore a double crown: the high white crown of Upper Egypt, combined with the red crown of Lower Egypt, as a sign that he ruled the two lands.

The long history of ancient Egypt is divided into three major periods—the Old, Middle, and New Kingdoms. Separating these were two Intermediate Periods. The Intermediate Periods were times of political and social upheaval, when the kingdom was not united. In the third century B.C. an Egyptian priest, Manetho, compiled a history of his land. He organized the kings of Egypt into thirty dynasties, or families of rulers. His system is used to this day.

The founding king of the First Dynasty of the united Egypt was, we believe, Menes who—Manetho wrote—ruled for 62 years and

This copy of a 3000 B.C. slate palette is a picture record of the birth of Egypt. King Narmer, wearing the high crown of the Upper Kingdom, is shown smiting the enemy—to become ruler of the united kingdom. The king's name appears in hieroglyphics between the horned heads at the top of the palette. The reverse side shows Narmer wearing the crown of Lower Egypt, and a pair of leopards form a hollow where pigment could be mixed.

As early as the Third Dynasty, Egyptian stone
sculptors were creating beautiful works.
The carving on the trial piece at the right shows
a king wearing the crown of Lower Egypt.

died after being wounded by a hippopotamus. He established a capital at Memphis, in Lower Egypt. Over the next 400 years, through the First and Second Dynasties, the model for the Egyptian state developed. The structure of government took shape and society began to separate into three layers—the ruler, who was believed to be a living god; the officials; and the peasants. The practical arts and crafts flourished, an art style developed, and the building of temples opened the way to later advances in architecture.

Beginning with the Third Dynasty, Egypt entered upon its first great period—the Old Kingdom, from about 2686 to 2160 B.C., Dynasties Three through Eight. The symbol of the Old Kingdom is the pyramid, a huge stone tomb built for the all-powerful ruler who in life was the god-king Horus, and in death became Osiris, the god of the dead. The first great stone tomb—the Step Pyramid—was built in the reign of King Djoser of the Third Dynasty. Kings of the Fourth Dynasty—Cheops (Khufu), Chephren, and Mycerinus—built huge, true pyramids.

The king had great power, and ruled over all areas of life through a large group of officials. The chief official was the vizier. The country was divided into about forty districts called nomes, each ruled by a governor, a nomarch, who was subject to the king.

For a long period Egypt flourished. Irrigation projects were built, copper mines and stone quarries developed, trade expeditions were sent to lands outside Egypt. Egypt was a strong, well-governed state, and the people lived in peace and plenty. But during the Sixth Dynasty, the nomarchs began to demand power and independence and the central government grew weak. Trade was upset, economic problems swelled, until the king could no longer rule. The nomes began to fight among themselves and the state collapsed. It was the end of the Old Kingdom.

THE MIDDLE KINGDOM

The fall of the Old Kingdom was followed by a time of chaos, famine, and disorder. It is called the First Intermediate Period, and it lasted from 2160 to 2040 B.C., from Dynasty Nine to Eleven. Gradually two rival centers of power emerged—one at Herakleopolis and one at Thebes. About 2040 B.C. the ruler of Thebes, Mentuhotpe II, conquered his rivals and reunited Egypt under one king. This marks the beginning of the Middle Kingdom, which lasted from 2040 to 1700 B.C., from late Dynasty Eleven through Thirteen. Mentuhotpe II made Thebes the new capital of Egypt, but in the Twelfth Dynasty, the capital was moved again, to a site near Memphis. Thebes had proven to be too far south to rule the whole country.

The Middle Kingdom was one of the most prosperous and brilliant periods in Egypt's history. The restored strong central government worked to strengthen the borders against outside enemies—Nubians, Libyans, and Asiatics. The Twelfth Dynasty kings ruled with absolute power.

To encourage trade, King Senwosret III had a canal dug around the First Cataract of the Nile, where it had been impossible for ships to navigate. He had another canal dug from the east branch of the Nile to the Red Sea. Trade with Punt (in the region of modern Eritrea), with Syria, Cyprus, and Crete was lively and profitable. Egypt conquered Nubia and made it a province.

The next ruler, Amenemhat III, sent his agents, known as "the Eyes and Ears of the King," throughout the kingdom. They watched and listened, and reported back to the king what the people were doing and thinking. They let him know whether people were hard at work, or whether they were dissatisfied and perhaps plotting against their ruler. And these agents made sure that the nomarchs, or provincial governors, sent the king his share of the taxes promptly.

Egypt established colonies and increased its farm lands by irrigating thousands of acres in an oasis just west of the Nile and south of Memphis. Today this area is known as the Fayum. Each year the overflow of the Nile passed through a natural cut in the hills into the Fayum, but the water receded as the river fell. The kings of the Twelfth Dynasty decided to save this water. They built dams and canals so that some of the water could be saved to irrigate the Fayum. The rest they released during the driest months for use farther down along the Nile.

THE NEW KINGDOM

During the Thirteenth Dynasty, under a long series of weak rulers, the central government again crumbled. The time of weakness and turmoil that followed is called the Second Intermediate Period, which lasted from 1700 to 1559 B.C., from the Fourteenth through Seventeenth Dynasties. Groups of foreign intruders, an Asiatic people Manetho called the Hyksos, took advantage of the weakness of the Egyptian rulers. With war chariots, horses, and bronze weapons—all new to the Egyptians—they seized control of the state and ruled for about a hundred years. At last, about 1567 B.C., the Theban king Ahmose drove the Hyksos out of Egypt.

Ahmose reunited the two kingdoms and became the first ruler of the New Kingdom or, as it is sometimes called, the Empire. The New Kingdom lasted from 1559 to 1085 B.C., from the Eighteenth through the Twentieth Dynasties. It was a 500-year period in which Egypt became the most powerful state in the ancient Near East. The capital was at Thebes.

While peace was soon restored and the economy recovered in the Eighteenth Dynasty, people were bitter over having been ruled by the foreign Hyksos. They wanted strong borders and security. The large and growing army influenced not only government policies, but also the lives and thoughts of the people. Egypt's frontiers, people said, must be extended as far as possible so that no enemy could invade and rule the country.

The king was once more the divine and absolute ruler. The ruler's chief support came from the priests, who were given rich gifts

Queen Hatshepsut built this splendid temple
into the base of the cliffs at Deir el Bahri. Inside,
wall carvings portray her great achievements.

and land. A tremendous governmental machinery, or bureaucracy, was developed to manage and direct the nomes, and oversee the collection of the crushing taxes.

Tuthmosis I, a ruler after Ahmose, chose a new burial ground in a valley to the west of Thebes. So many rulers were later buried there that it came to be known as the "Valley of the Kings." Tuthmosis did not want robbers to enter his tomb, and thought that he had chosen a place that would always remain a secret.

When Tuthmosis III came to the throne, in 1504 B.C., he was still a child. His co-ruler and stepmother Hatshepsut soon took all power from him and proclaimed herself king. After her death in 1482 B.C., Tuthmosis regained power and began a long series of campaigns to expand Egypt's territory. Under his rule, the Egyptian Empire extended from Mesopotamia to the Fourth Cataract of the Nile. The mighty pharaoh demanded a rich tribute of horses, slaves, gold, silver, and timber from the conquered peoples.

Under the magnificent rulers of the great Eighteenth Dynasty, Egypt became a powerful state. Princes from various parts of the empire were brought to Egypt and educated. Then they went home to their provinces to rule as servants of the pharaoh. Ties with other countries were strengthened and peace was insured by the pharaoh's custom of marrying native princesses.

In spite of all this, however, there were troubles in the empire. The rich were growing richer, the poor, poorer. The captives, brought from conquered lands to work for Egypt, were restless.

Several hundred interesting letters addressed to the pharaoh have been discovered at a place that today is called Tell el Amarna. They are all from foreign states and are written on clay tablets. We do not have the pharaoh's replies, but they were probably written on papyri. The letters give us a vivid glimpse of the peoples that made up the New Kingdom world. The diplomatic correspondence has to do with the Babylonians and Assyrians, the Hittites of Asia Minor, the people of Cyprus, and the Minoans of Crete, who are spoken of as living on the Isles of the Sea. It was a large and civilized world and its products, from Greece to Nubia and Punt, poured into Egypt.

DAILY LIFE IN EGYPT

Through the long history of ancient Egypt, the daily life of the people followed the same patterns. Old beliefs and traditional ways of doing things were treasured; the people and their rulers honored their past and tried to hold to it. An important Egyptian idea was a belief in the spirit of *ma'at*—a sense of harmony, truth, and order in the natural world. In the concept of *ma'at*, things are right if they are the way they should be; and that is set by the way things were in the past. Even when society was upset by turmoil in the Intermediate Periods, the people tried to put everything back the way it had been as soon as they could. So the picture of Egyptian life we build up from papyri, tomb paintings, literature, and historical reports shows life as it generally was—through the Old, Middle, and New Kingdoms.

At the head of the society was the king. In the New Kingdom, the rulers adopted the title of "pharaoh," which meant "great house" or "palace." Now it is often used for the earlier kings, too. The upper class of Egyptian society was made up of government officials, nobles, and priests. The middle class included skilled workers, scribes, artists, teachers, soldiers, tradespeople, and other city dwellers. The peasants, who were mostly farmworkers, laborers, or servants, made up the largest class. At the bottom of society were the slaves. This was a small group because slavery was not common in ancient Egypt, especially before the New Kingdom. Nearly all the slaves in Egypt were foreign captives.

The king lived in a large and luxurious palace. In early times and through the Old Kingdom, the king's capital was at Memphis.

Some later kings ruled from Thebes. Surrounding the palace were temples, official buildings, and the houses of the nobles. These houses were not as large as we might expect. Memphis and Thebes, like all Egyptian cities, were built near the river—the chief means of transportation and communication, and the source of water. Since the only land fit for use was that near the river, as much as possible was kept for farming. Living space was limited.

In the towns and cities houses were crowded close together and faced directly onto the street, with very small gardens in the back. A noble's house was usually two or three stories high. Nearly all buildings—except temples, which were meant to last forever—were made of sun-dried mud brick. The family slept on an upper story at the back of the house, where it was quiet. Servants slept on the ground floor next to the noisy street.

The nobles' large country houses were very different. They were spreading, one-story buildings, with courtyards and porches that overlooked shady gardens and pools filled with lilies and fish. The servants lived in separate buildings to the rear.

The homes of the wealthy were furnished with splendid furniture made of ebony and other rare woods, ivory, silver, and other metals. There were folding stools, chairs, and tables. Woven rush mats covered the floors. At night, the rooms were lit by bowls or dishes of oil with floating wicks. Beds were built to slope down from the head to the foot, and had footboards so the sleeper would not slip down too far. Strands of cord served as bedsprings, with layers of folded linen sheets as mattresses. Wooden headrests were commonly used, even by those who did not have beds.

A stone sculpture shows a noble couple of the New Kingdom—the chief royal secretary and his wife.

The servants cooked the family's dinners in the servants' quarters. They had fires of wood or charcoal and used kettles and other utensils much like those we use today. The nobles ate from dishes of pottery, or alabaster, or even of copper, bronze, or gold, and, in later days, colorful glass. The meals were large and varied. They dined on milk, bread, fish, poultry, meat, vegetables, and fruit and used honey for sweetening. They drank beer and wine. Beer was very popular among all groups. It was made from the same dough as bread. After the dough was prepared, kneaded, and left to rise, the loaves were either baked into bread or else mixed with water and allowed to ferment into beer.

Both men and women of the nobility often wore wigs and jewelry, and used cosmetics made from minerals. Creams and oils were rubbed into the skin to prevent sun-drying; women outlined their eyes with kohl (a black powder from lead ore) and colored their cheeks and lips with red ocher. Men shaved with bronze razors. They wore linen skirts—a straight piece of cloth wrapped around the body—and left their chests bare, or wore linen shirts. Women wore long, straight linen dresses. Both men and women wore sandals of woven rushes, or leather, but most often walked barefoot.

A noble woman had her name written in ink on all her household linens. Other valuables were kept in jars, baskets, and chests marked with her seal. The seals would not keep thieves out, but would alert the owners that something had been stolen.

The Egyptians, rich and poor, seem to have had happy family lives. Paintings and sculpture and literature give evidence of affection and warmth. The pharaoh was allowed more than one wife at a time; but most Egyptians married just once. Marriage seems to have been a partnership, and wives enjoyed freedom and respect.

Egyptian children played with all sorts of toys: wooden animals with movable jaws, dolls, rattles, small axes, and more. They often had pets: cats, dogs, monkeys or baboons, and sometimes gazelles. They ran, jumped, played games, and swam; while

[18]

The Egyptians fished and hunted water birds
from boats such as this painted wooden model
found in a Middle Kingdom tomb.

adults enjoyed bullfights, threw knuckle bones (in place of dice), and played the popular board game, *senet*.

Magicians, storytellers, wrestlers, dancers, and musicians provided entertainment for the whole family. The Egyptians were very fond of music. Professionals and amateurs played harps, lutes and flutes, oboes, and clarinets.

The favorite sports of the Egyptians were fishing and hunting. These often provided food as well as pleasure. The Egyptians fished from the banks of the Nile, or from boats, using nets, hooks, and spears.

The Egyptians also enjoyed trapping birds, or bringing them down with boomerangs. Cats were used to retrieve the game, just as dogs are used today. When hunters set off for bigger game, such as wild cattle, hyenas, and the lions and elephants that lived in the desert, they carried spears and bows and arrows and brought along several good hunting dogs.

Right beside the Nile, the Egyptians hunted hippopotamuses and crocodiles. Herodotus, a Greek historian of the fifth century B.C. who visited Egypt, described the most common way of hunting crocodiles: "The Egyptians bait a hook with a cut of pork and let it float out into the middle of the river. The hunter sits on the bank and beats a living pig. The crocodile hears its cries and going in the direction of the noise, meets the pork and immediately swallows it. The men on shore pull in the line, and when they have landed the crocodile, the first thing they do is plaster its eyes with mud. Then they kill the animal easily; otherwise it gives much trouble."

Parents took special pains to teach both boys and girls manners, but when it came to formal education, they favored the boys. The highest purpose of education was to prepare a boy for a post in the government. If a boy's ambition was little lower, he might hope to become a scribe—an official clerk, or writer. Scribes were important members of the Egyptian middle class and often acted as teachers.

Whatever his aim in life, the first thing a boy learned was to read and write. He memorized proverbs and practiced writing model letters that he might use later on. Then he learned arithmetic and geometry. Mathematics was necessary because he might get a job keeping tax lists, and every imaginable thing was taxed to support the government. Or he might get a job of surveying the land and recording boundaries after the overflow of the Nile had swept away the landmarks of the year before. An educated Egyptian could rise from a lower class to a higher. This freedom was healthy for the country as it encouraged new life and ideas in the society.

The life of the poor was in sharp contrast to the luxurious life of the nobles. Poor Egyptians lived in mud huts that were crowded together along narrow, crooked lanes. Their clothing was a single linen garment, and their food consisted of bread, vegetables, beans, lentils, and fish.

The mother of the family was respected. She looked after the children, fetched water from the well or the river, ground meal between two stones, baked bread in the ashes of a wood fire, sewed, spun thread, and wove cloth.

The father's day was spent in the field or at his job. If he worked as a carpenter, he used tools much like our own—mallets, axes, knives, chisels, and saws.

There was other work for the peasants, too. In the days of the Old Kingdom, there was no standing army. The king ordered local governors to call up troops—mostly from among the peasants—when trouble loomed. Later rulers had large, well-organized armies and professional soldiers. Officers came from the nobility and the commercial middle class of the cities. The peasants were also called upon to work on state projects—canals, pyramids, temples. This work was usually planned for the flood season, when they could not work the fields.

FARMING AND TRADE

The Nile River and the hard-working peasant-farmers together supported the life of ancient Egypt. The peasants were not slaves; they were free tenant farmers who worked land that was the property of the pharaoh, or a noble, or a temple. They kept a small share of the crop as wages and paid their rent and taxes with the products of the farm.

There were no horses in Egypt until the New Kingdom, and no camels until much later, but many other animals roamed the countryside and grazed in swampy areas. Donkeys, pigs, oxen, sheep, goats, ducks, and geese were abundant. Date palms, and pomegranate, olive, and fig trees grew in the fields. There were beautiful flower gardens, and many Egyptians kept bees to supply the honey they liked for sweetening foods and drinks.

The farming calendar was set by the Nile. There were three seasons, each divided into four months. The "inundation" or flood season, when the Nile overflowed and covered most of the land in the Nile Valley and the Delta, lasted from June through September. Next was the season of "going out," when the fields emerged from the water. This season began in October and lasted until about February. The season of drought was the harvest season, from February to June. Then the cycle began again.

During the flood season, the peasants worked on state projects. Then, as soon as the waters receded, they went back to the land with their wooden plows and baskets of seed. One worker scattered seed, while one or two others guided a team of cows or oxen hitched to a plow that looked like a hoe with a long handle point-ing forward. After the plowing was finished, herds of pigs and sheep were driven over the ground to trample in the seeds. Then the surface was smoothed with a wooden rake.

Egyptian farmers grew barley, a wheat called emmer, pulses (lentils and chickpeas), vegetables and beans, flax for linen, sesame plants for their oil, grapes, and other fruits.

At harvest time all the peasants gathered in the fields. The men cut the grain with bronze sickles and threshed it by driving the cattle over it. The women gathered corn or other crops.

Agriculture was truly the basis of the economy in Egypt. There was no coined money; people traded or bartered for the goods they needed, offering a certain amount of grain, for example, for a cow or a bed.

Egypt traded actively through the ancient world, here too using a barter system to bring back the goods it wanted. Ships sailed from Egypt northwest to islands in the Aegean Sea, northeast to Palestine, Phoenicia, Syria, and to Asia Minor, south to Nubia and along the coast of Africa. They brought back spices and incense, ebony, ivory, and gold. From the nearby Sinai Peninsula they obtained copper. Egypt had plenty of stone for building, but there were few trees for wood. For that reason the Egyptian traders traveled to Syria to barter for the fine "cedars of Lebanon," which they brought back to Egypt on barges.

In exchange for these things, the Egyptians exported grain and papyrus; beautiful jewelry of gold, silver, and copper; nearly transparent stone vases; exquisite furniture; fine linen tapestries. The craftsworkers of ancient Egypt rank with the very best in his-tory.

Over: in this wall painting from a New Kingdom tomb, workers harvest crops while inspectors use ropes to measure the fields and scribes record the figures.

RELIGION

Every part of life in Egypt—birth and death, the flooding of the Nile, the rising of the sun—was subject to the gods. Religion spread through all of life.

In the early days, the people worshiped the forces of nature. As towns grew, each had its own set of gods, often shown in animal form, or later, with an animal head. Horus, falcon-headed god of light, was worshiped in one part of the delta; Hathor, cow-headed goddess of love or women, ruled in Memphis; Thoth, god of wisdom who was worshiped in another part of the delta, appeared as an ibis or a baboon. Some of these gods— Re, the sun god; Nut, goddess of the sky; Horus and others— came to be gods of all the people. Others remained local gods. New gods arose at different periods, and some gods took on greater importance, or different responsibilities. In Thebes, Amun, god of air, was worshiped. When Thebes became the center of Egypt, Amun was joined to the sun god Re, and the new god Amun-Re was worshiped.

The festivals in honor of the gods provided holidays for the people. There were plays telling the story of the god who was being honored. The plays told how the god had suffered and then at last had overcome enemies and misfortunes. A figure of the god in a holy boat would be carried in procession by the priests, to the accompaniment of music and dancing.

Although all life in Egypt depended on the Nile, the Egyptians believed that the sun was the true source of life. When the sun

Anubis, god of the dead and guardian of tombs,
was portrayed with the head of a jackal.

disappeared in the evening, it suggested death. When it rose again in the morning, it suggested rebirth and a new life. The Nile, too, suggested rebirth, for every year it renewed life with its overflow. This influenced the Egyptians in one of their strongest beliefs—that when they died they would be reborn.

The king of the dead and immortality, or everlasting life, was Osiris. He was god of the underworld and sat at the judgment seat with his wife-sister, Isis, to decide whether a spirit entering the next world had belonged in life to a good person or a bad one. If the spirit was judged to have belonged to a good person, it would be given eternal happiness. If its owner had been bad, it would be turned over to a monster to be devoured. For this reason, the Egyptians spent a large part of their time preparing their souls for the next world. And if people were rich and powerful, there was still another reason for wanting to prepare for the next world—life on earth was so delightful that they wanted to prolong it after death.

The Egyptians believed that the tomb, or burial place, served as a bridge between life and death. Therefore they stored food and drink in it to keep the spirit alive. They painted cheerful pictures of daily life on the walls, and these pictures had to include food and drink so that the spirit would not have to leave the tomb when it had eaten all the real provisions.

Because the Egyptians thought the body had to serve as a home for the soul after death, they believed they must preserve the body as long as possible. The dry climate of Egypt helped, but not indefinitely. To preserve dead bodies, the Egyptians embalmed, or mummified, them.

The carefully prepared, wrapped mummy was placed inside a painted wooden coffin.

Herodotus, the historian of ancient Greece, described how the Egyptians did this. "First," he wrote, "the Egyptians take a crooked piece of iron and draw the brains out through the nostrils, thus getting rid of some of it, while the skull is cleared of the rest by rinsing with drugs. Then they make an incision in the flank with a sharp stone and take out the entrails. Next, they cleanse the body and wash it with palm-wine. After this, they fill the body with myrrh, with cassia, and every other sort of spice, except frankincense, and sew up the opening.

"Then the body is soaked in saltpeter for forty days. The body is next washed once more and wrapped round with strips of fine linen. This is smeared over with gum. In this state the body is given back to the relatives, who enclose it in a wooden case, which they have made for the purpose, shaped in the figure of a man. Then fastening the case, they place it in the tomb, upright against the wall."

Poor people were buried quite simply, but the nobles were laid to rest in large, flat-topped rectangular tombs called mastabas. These clustered about the pyramids of the king, so that the nobles might continue to serve him in death and share his immortality.

THE PYRAMIDS

King Djoser, a ruler of the Third Dynasty of the Old Kingdom, was served by a remarkable vizier, or chief official, Imhotep. Imhotep was overseer of works, architect, engineer, advisor, and master physician. In later centuries, he was honored as the god of medicine. But he is best known for the huge stone tomb he is said to have designed for his king. Imhotep copied, in stone, the mud-brick mastabas (bench-shaped tombs) that had served for burials of earlier kings. He built a series of six graduated mastabas, placed one on top of the other, to create a 204 foot (62.18 m) towering structure at Saqqara, the royal burial ground near Memphis. This tomb, which we call a step pyramid because each mastaba created a huge step, was the first large structure built all of stone, and the first pyramid in Egypt. Imhotep's step pyramid led from the old tradition of mastaba burials to a new one of pyramid tombs. This became the pattern for the Old Kingdom and for later periods, too.

Surrounding the pyramid was a small city of related buildings—shrines, altars, temples, storage rooms, courts, and tombs for nobles.

The Fourth Dynasty (2613 to 2498 B.C.) is called the Age of Pyramids. Three great kings of this period—Cheops, Chephren, and Mycerinus—each built a towering, tremendous structure to house his mummy. The pyramids stand on the edge of the desert not far from Memphis, to the west of the Nile at modern Giza. The largest, the Great Pyramid of Cheops, covers 13 acres (5.2 ha). Two

The step pyramid built by Imhotep for King Djoser,
ruler of the Third Dynasty, was the first
all-stone structure. The restored buildings in front
of the pyramid were part of the temple complex.

and a half million blocks of stone were used, and the average weight of the blocks was about 2.5 tons (2.3 m.t.).

The Great Pyramid represents an amazing architectural and engineering feat. Iron was unknown at the time, so the Egyptians had tools only of stone, copper, or bronze. The block and tackle and the pulley were not yet in use, so the great blocks of stone were lifted into place by means of ropes, levers, and rollers.

We have not yet discovered all the details of the building of the Great Pyramid, but we do have a general understanding of how it was done. The king chose a place for the pyramid on the edge of the desert, but beyond the harmful reach of the Nile's overflow.

The site was solid rock. This was leveled off, and then the work was started. The base of the pyramid was about 755 feet (229 m) on each side. The blocks that went into the construction of the core of the great burial place were quarried nearby. As the pyramid rose, mud-brick ramps were built against its sides so that more and more blocks could be hauled into place. The pyramid was actually built in a series of steps, and it grew narrower as it rose. There are 137 steps, or courses, as they are called. The total height of Cheops' Pyramid is 481 feet (146 m).

Once the courses had been laid, the Egyptians faced the great structure with finer white limestone blocks that had been quarried east of the Nile and ferried across the river. The Egyptians did this when the river's overflow was at its height so that the rafts could come as close as possible to the site of the pyramid.

Workers unloaded the blocks and dragged them on rollers along a stone causeway, or road, that had been built right up to the pyramid. After the facing blocks were set in place, the pyramid was absolutely smooth from top to bottom. The blocks fitted to a fiftieth of an inch. There was no need to secure them with mortar, with precision such as this. Most of these blocks were stolen by looters in later ages. That is why the pyramid today has its stepped appearance.

The ruler was especially anxious that robbers should not find his actual tomb, so it was placed deep inside the pyramid. From a

King Chephren's huge Sphinx, seen here with
the Great Pyramid in the background, guarded
the road to the king's temple.

hidden door on the north side, a 156-foot (47-m) passageway goes down, then winds upward to the king's tomb. On the way it passes the queen's tomb and various chapels for the worship of the royal pair's spirits.

When the time came to close up the pyramid, the doors of the king's and queen's tombs were sealed, and huge blocks were rolled into the passageway. Nevertheless, thieves did break in and steal the contents of the tombs. The most important thing they left behind was the plain, granite sarcophagus that originally held Cheops' body. It was too big to carry away.

Near this great pyramid stood temples and the mastabas of the nobles. Chephren and Mycerinus also built their pyramids here. Like Cheops, they built them during their own lifetimes because they were unwilling to trust anyone else to attend to their souls' resting places.

King Chephren built the famous Sphinx beside his pyramid. The head of the Sphinx is a portrait of himself, 66 feet (20 m) high, but the body is that of a lion to suggest the king's great strength and power.

In building these huge structures, the rulers of the Fourth Dynasty used a great amount of natural resources, and the wealth of the kingdom, and the hard labor of their subjects. None of the kings who came later could match them. In his description of the pyramids Herodotus writes: "There is an inscription in Egyptian characters on the pyramid that gives the amount of radishes, onions, and garlic used by the laborers. I remember the interpreter who translated for me saying that the money spent in this way was 1,600 talents of silver (1 talent = $1,800). If this is correct, what a huge amount must have gone for the tools and for the feeding and clothing of the workers."

THE TOMB OF TUTANKHAMUN

Tombs were meant to be sacred resting places for the rulers of Egypt. But the treasures they held were tempting lures for thieves, and they were often plundered—sometimes soon after the royal burial.

At the start of the New Kingdom, the pharaohs selected a new burial ground, perhaps trying to find safety from thieves. They ordered tombs cut into the rock walls of a remote valley (later called the Valley of Kings) in the desert west of Thebes. Here, until the capital was moved from Thebes about 1085 B.C., the kings were buried. But these tombs, too, were broken into and sacked.

In 1922, an English archeologist, Howard Carter, made a marvelous discovery—the nearly untouched tomb of a New Kingdom pharaoh named Tutankhamun who had ruled Egypt in the fourteenth century B.C. Other tombs that had been found had been stripped of the treasures placed in them for the king's use in the next world. Carter's discovery provided the first chance to see an intact funeral shrine and mummy of a pharaoh, and it also demonstrated how archeology adds to our knowledge of the past.

For years Carter had been excavating in the Valley of the Kings, hoping to find the entrance to a royal tomb. He was nearly ready to give up when his workers uncovered steps cut into the rock floor. They led to a plastered-over door.

There were signs that thieves had managed to break through

The gold panel from the back of King Tutankhamun's
throne shows a brilliantly colored scene
of the queen anointing the young ruler.

the door, but it had then been resealed by royal officials. And imprinted in the door were seals bearing the name Tutankhamun who ruled from about 1334 to 1325 B.C. With great excitement Carter made a small hole in the door and looked through. All he could see was a passage filled with rubble, but nothing else. He re-covered the doorway, assigned guards for the night, and went back to his camp to sleep.

Finally the work began. Passages, stairways, and sealed doorways were opened and cleared until at last the workers came to what seemed to be the final chamber. A small hole was made in the door, and one of the workers held a lighted candle in front of it. But instead of the foul gases that were expected, hot air rushed out of the hole. When Carter looked through it, he could see nothing at first except gold. Gold was everywhere. Then slowly he made out the forms of animals and statues, couches, beautiful alabaster vases, chairs, chariots, golden bouquets of flowers, and a throne. The throne was covered with sheet gold and decorated with glass of many colors, earthenware, and stone inlay.

One thing, however, Carter did not see. That was a mummy or a coffin. He realized that this was merely an antechamber, and that the greatest discoveries still lay ahead.

The work continued until the burial chamber itself was reached, and Carter drew back the bolts of the door. There, filling the room, was what seemed to be a wall of gold. It was one side of a gilded shrine, 17 feet (5.15 m) long, 11 feet (3.33 m) wide, and 9 feet (2.73 m) high. This was the first of four golden shrines, one inside the other. The shrines enclosed a great stone sarcophagus. This, in turn, enclosed a nest of three coffins, the first two of gilded wood and the last of solid gold. Within the gold coffin lay the mummy of the young king, wearing a gold mask.

Tutankhamun's innermost coffin was made of solid gold.

Tutankhamun's body had been carefully mummified and wrapped in fine linen. But so many oils had been poured on it during the last ceremonies, that the body had decomposed much more than those of most Egyptian mummies.

THE ROSETTA STONE

For nearly fifteen centuries, the beautiful Egyptian writing system had mystified the world. Until the fourth century A.D., Egyptian priests had used hieroglyphics and guarded their secrets; then their meanings had been lost. A fortunate discovery by troops of Napoleon of France produced the key to the mystery.

In 1799 French soldiers on an expedition in Egypt unearthed a piece of black basalt stone, 3.75 feet (1.14 m) long, 2 feet 4 inches (711 mm) wide, and 11 inches (279 mm) thick. It was found near the Rosetta mouth of the Nile River. Today this "Rosetta Stone" is one of the treasures of the British Museum.

The front of the stone consisted of three sections, each covered with a different form of writing. The bottom section was written in Greek, and scholars were able to read that easily. They found it was a decree issued in 196 B.C., honoring the ruler of Egypt, Ptolemy V. After praising Ptolemy's deeds, it ordered that copies of the decree be engraved on stone tables in both Greek and Egyptian, and placed in temples throughout the land. This was proof of what scholars had guessed by inspecting the stone—the three panels all held the same text, written in three scripts. The top panel was hieroglyphics, the ancient form of Egyptian priestly writing. The center panel was another Egyptian script, demotic— the simpler, popular form of writing that was in use at the time of Ptolemy. Scholars throughout the world were now certain that the Greek text could be used to decipher the hieroglyphics. But

Hieroglyphic inscriptions appear throughout
the ancient Egyptian world—on papyri,
on temples, obelisks, and in tombs,
as seen across the top of this wall carving
showing death offerings.

the task was not as easy as they expected. It took over twenty years. The first progress was made when scholars noticed the hieroglyphics section had five ovals containing identical sets of symbols. The Greek text mentioned the king's name five times. By guessing that the five ovals held Ptolemy's name, they made the first step toward deciphering the text. The ovals, which occur in nearly all Egyptian inscriptions, came to be called cartouches, because the French soldiers thought their shape was the same as that of their gun cartridges, or cartouches.

After many more years of work and study of inscriptions on other monuments, a young French scholar, Jean Francois Champollion, was able to claim in 1822 that he had finally deciphered the Egyptian writing system. He had learned that the Egyptians used symbols that stood for letters, and many more symbols that were signs for combinations of two or three letters, and also picture symbols that stood for words or ideas. Since his time, the inscriptions, papyri and other records holding the stories, history, and beliefs of the Egyptians are open to us.

ARCHITECTURE, LITERATURE, AND SCIENCE

The grandeur of Egyptian architecture can be seen in the stone temples as well as in the pyramids. The Egyptian style developed early, and most of its characteristics can be seen in Old Kingdom structures: flat roofs, mud brick for domestic buildings and stone for sacred structures, huge walls covered with carved hieroglyphics and pictures. Mastabas, pyramids, obelisks, and pylons appear in nearly all Egyptian sites.

Temples were built as homes for the gods and places for the performance of the god's rituals. Other temples were funeral monuments for dead rulers. The basic features of the temples were the same, although they varied by size and ground plan. Every ruler built temples, or added onto those built earlier. They were large, walled, one-level structures, built of limestone. The entrance was through a pylon (from the Greek word for gate), or gateway—a pair of sloping, flat-topped towers flanking an entranceway. The pylon led into an open courtyard with colonnades along the sides. This court led to the hypostyle (from the Greek for "resting on pillars"), a great central columned hall. The column tops—the capitals—were often carved in the shape of papyrus flowers. The hypostyle was where rituals were performed. Beyond it was the sanctuary, or sacred area, for the god of the temple.

Carved and painted on the temple walls were pictures of the great deeds of the pharaoh who had built it. Outside the temple stood obelisks—four-sided stone pillars that tapered from the

**The ram was sacred to the god Amun,
and so, ram-headed sphinxes lined the road
to the Temple of Amun at Karnak.**

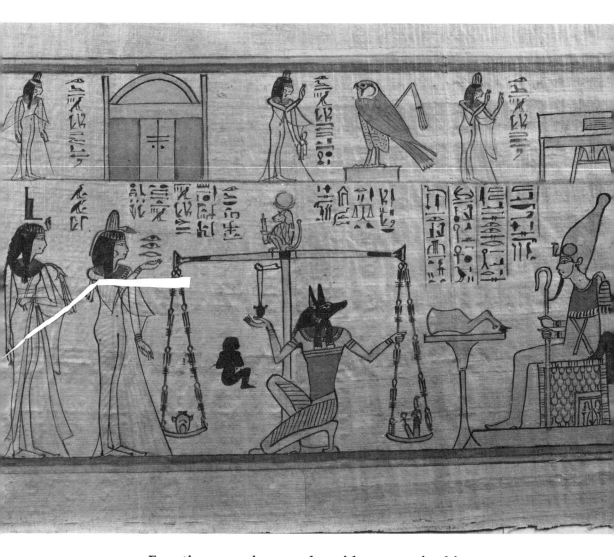

Egyptian papyri covered a wide range of subjects—history, medicine, magic, and religion. This papyrus from a royal tomb at Thebes shows the jackal-headed god Anubis weighing the heart of a dead person to determine whether it is pure or evil.

base to the top, and ended in a pyramid shape. They too were covered with a carved record of the pharaoh's deeds. Surrounding the temple were storerooms, workshops, homes for the priests and more, all making up a temple complex.

Two of the most famous Egyptian temples date from the New Kingdom: the Temple of Amun at Karnak, near Thebes, and the funeral temple built by Queen Hatshepsut at Deir el Bahri, in the Valley of the Kings.

Because the Egyptians had a system of writing, they could create a record of their lives and their achievements. And also, they could create a literature. Poems, stories, essays, narratives, and myths were preserved on papyrus, not just in the memory of the people.

Egyptian literature shows the people to be lively, interested in all forms of knowledge, and responsive. There is a wide range of works, most often by unknown authors. There are love songs and poems, accounts of the creation of the world, stories of the gods, historical narratives, observations of the world, and tales of travel and adventure. One story is very like that of Sinbad. It tells of a sailor who was shipwrecked on an island in the Red Sea and, after many adventures, finally returned home.

One popular kind of writing in all periods of ancient Egypt is called "wisdom literature." Here an older, wise person gives advice to the young. There were also many religious texts, and tombs usually held a copy of "The Book of the Dead," a collection of spells and charms. This also included a description of the next world and warnings of the monsters the dead may meet there, and poems and hymns to the gods.

The Egyptians were a practical people, and to them knowledge was important because it was useful. They needed ways to measure their fields, and predict the size of their crops, and figure out supplies, so they created a simple arithmetic and geometry. They learned to survey land as property boundaries had to be relocated after the Nile's overflow every year. They developed engineering and numerical skills in building the pyramids. Their concern with religion and the need for arranging a calendar of festivals led to their interest in astronomy. By careful observation, they learned the movements of some stars, and charted the skies.

One of their greatest achievements was their creation of a calendar that is the basis of our modern calendar. They set the beginning of the year on the day the Nile began to rise (about July 19 by our calendar), for this was the most important event. Astronomers noticed that this occurred at the same time the brightest star in the sky—Sirius, the Dog Star—rose with the sun. By counting the number of days until the Dog Star again rose at dawn, they worked out a calendar of 365 days. They learned they needed to correct the calendar every so often by adding extra days, as we add a day in leap years.

The Egyptians also divided day and night into twelve parts (hours) each, and they created shadow clocks that marked the time by the shadow cast by an upright arm onto a horizontal arm, and water clocks. In these, the passing of time was measured by water dripping out of a hole at the bottom of a stone bowl.

The Egyptians were also especially interested in the practical science of medicine. Some scholars honor them with the title of the first real doctors. Their medicine was a mixture of science, religion, and magic; thus the people who were doctors were often priests as well. They used medical treatments along with spells and rituals, for they thought that evil spirits caused disease. They studied anatomy and were the first to discover that the pulse had something to do with the heart's beat. A number of medical papyri have been found, including one that dates from the Old Kingdom and is perhaps the work of Imhotep, King Djoser's vizier, architect, and physician. It is a study of the heart, and describes conditions and treatment. Other papyri are textbooks on how to treat physical injuries, how to splint broken bones, stitch cuts, and heal burns. Superstitions, spells, and charms are included, too.

The Egyptians also used many drugs, made from herbs, minerals, and natural substances. Their fame as doctors spread beyond Egypt, and they traveled to Persia, Syria, and other lands.

A REVOLUTIONARY PHARAOH

Toward the end of the Eighteenth Dynasty, about 1353 B.C., Amenhotpe IV became ruler of Egypt. This pharaoh's attention did not center on empire building. The young pharaoh thought it wrong that the government should completely control the lives of the people. He also thought the priests should not have the power to tell the people what they must think and believe. The vast Egyptian empire in his reign stretched from Mesopotamia to the Nile, and included many different kinds of people. But Amenhotpe believed that all people were similar. This led him to think of one god who could be the same for all people, everywhere. Gradually, Amenhotpe adopted as his god Aton—the life-giving sun who affected all people, everywhere.

Amenhotpe set out to destroy the religion of the old god, Amun, and his priests. He changed his name to Akhenaton, which means "Aton be pleased." He forbade the worship of old gods, and ordered the people to worship him as god-king and the son of Aton, and through him, Aton—the one, universal god. He moved the capital north from Thebes, the center of the old religion, to the new city he built, Akhetaton, near the modern Tell el Amarna. The time of his rule is often called the Amarna Period.

Akhenaton's new religion brought new ideas to Egypt. With new ideas came a freedom of expression, particularly in the arts. Instead of portraying people in the old, formal style, artists now portrayed them in natural and lifelike poses.

One of the finest of all Egyptian portraits is a painted, limestone head of Akhenaton's wife, Nafertiti, found at Tell el Amarna.

Today it is one of the treasures of the Berlin Museum. In the Cairo Museum there is a beautiful limestone relief that shows Akhenaton and Nafertiti together. They are worshiping the Sun Disk, symbol of their god, Aton.

Akhenaton was so busy with religious reforms that he did not notice that his officials were oppressing the people. Moreover, the powerful Hittites of Asia Minor were expanding, and there were rumblings of war along Egypt's frontiers. When Akhenaton died, the Egyptians returned to their old worship of many gods and to the ways of the past. The capital was changed back again to Thebes.

Akhenaton and Nafertiti present offerings to the Sun Disk, symbol of their god, Aton, in this stone carving from Tell el Amarna.

THE RAMESSIDE AGE

While Akhenaton was concerned with religious, artistic, and social reforms, the empire was neglected. The return to old ways, after Akhenaton's death, did not solve Egypt's problems immediately. The rulers who followed concentrated on trying to put internal affairs back in order and neglected to guard the country's frontiers.

It was left to the Nineteenth and Twentieth Dynasties to restore the empire. This period is called the Ramesside Age (1303-1085 B.C.) because eleven of its pharaohs took the name Ramesses. These rulers erased all traces of Akhenaton, regained Egyptian possessions and trade routes, and restored prosperity.

Ramesses II brought magnificence back to Egypt. But in this era of building it seemed that all that mattered was size. Ramesses built a temple at Abu Simbel, far up the Nile. On each side he placed pairs of statues of himself, each about 67 feet (20.4 m) high. He had his own name placed on earlier rulers' statues, and even had their faces carved to look like his own. To make his buildings more magnificent, he carried away parts or furnishings of other buildings.

At Thebes, Ramesses built an enormous temple known as the Ramesseum, 590 feet (179.8 m) long by 180 feet (54.9 m) wide. And at Karnak he built a temple that is one of the largest buildings in the world, 1,215 feet (370 m) long and 376 feet (114.6 m) wide. The columns of the central hall are so huge that a hundred people could stand on the top of one.

**A colossal statue of Ramesses II
lies toppled beside the proud ruler's
enormous temple, the Ramesseum.**

Ramesses was a strong ruler. He fought off many invading groups and led an army north to win back Syria from the Hittites. At Kadesh, on the Orontes River, he was ambushed by the Hittites. He rallied his forces with fierce courage and cut his way out. Though the battle was far from a victory, he proudly recorded it on the walls of various temples in Egypt.

Shortly after, Ramesses and the Hittite king, Hattushilish III, drew up a peace treaty. Two copies of this treaty have been found in Egypt, and another among the ancient public records of the Hittite capital in Asia Minor. The document called thousands of gods to witness. It then divided Syria between the Egyptian and Hittite rulers, renewed previous treaties, and arranged for the two countries to defend each other in case of attack.

An interesting clause in the treaty is one calling for the surrender by each state of the refugees of the other and guaranteeing their decent treatment when they returned home. It emphasizes a sense of humanity we can appreciate.

THE FALL OF EGYPT

The wars with the Hittites weakened Egypt, and through the Nineteenth and into the Twentieth Dynasties other groups, including Libyans and Sea Peoples, began to press against Egypt. The last important pharaoh was Ramesses III who ruled from 1198 to 1166 B.C. By this time, however, the Egyptians had lost the will to fight. They had given over the protection of their country to paid foreign soldiers, or mercenaries. This was expensive and dangerous. Mercenaries cannot always be depended on in an emergency. Another terrible burden was the support of the numberless priests, their many temples and great tracts of land.

Added to these troubles inside the country, the threats on Egypt's frontiers were growing. These were days of great tribal upheavals and migrations. Barbarians overwhelmed the Hittites. In the western corner of Asia Minor, Greeks battered at the walls of Troy. The Philistines occupied the coast of Palestine. And in 1085 B.C., Libyans and other foreigners seized Egypt. The New Kingdom, and with it Egypt's long and great period in history, came to an end.

THE LEGACY OF EGYPT

The two thousand years of Egypt's history—from the time of King Narmer to the fall of the New Kingdom—offers us important lessons and a rich legacy.

One of the most dramatic lessons we can see in ancient Egypt is how amazingly long an autocratic state can last, even when faced by many enemies. Although the lives of the ordinary people were often difficult, they obeyed and honored their ruler, whom they believed to be both human and divine. They felt that the pharaoh guarded them against the injustices of officials and took their parts in disputes with the gods.

The history of Egypt also shows how rigidly clinging to the ways of the past stifles creativity. Many of the Egyptians' original ideas and advances were developed in the earliest times, in the days of the Old Kingdom. Later periods were more conservative and bound by tradition. The reforms of Akhenaton eased the tight limits on Egyptian life and activity. Art and architecture especially showed new energy and beauty during his time. Akhenaton's death, however, saw a return to the old ways.

But whatever weaknesses we may find, this ancient people occupy a most important place in the history of world civilization. It was the Egyptians who created what may have been the first great state, with a central government and the political machinery to rule a large population scattered throughout a wide area.

The Egyptian state was perhaps the first to plan and carry out large projects—such as dams and canal systems—to benefit many

A sculptured head of Ramesses II dominates
the court of the Temple of Luxor.

people. They developed a way of life that included work and the fulfillment of duties to the state and their religion. They were able to spend time at leisure and in creative activities.

Their many other marvelous achievements—their system of writing and the invention of writing material, their splendid furniture and wall paintings and sculptures of great beauty and sensitivity, their literature, religion, calendar, engineering marvels, arithmetic and record-keeping, medicine and more—form a magnificent legacy from a gifted people.

A TIMETABLE OF ANCIENT EGYPT*

3100 B.C.	Unification of Upper and Lower Egypt	
3100–2686 B.C.	Early Dynastic Period	Dynasties 1,2
2686–2160 B.C.	Old Kingdom	Dynasties 3–8
2160–2040 B.C.	First Intermediate Period	Dynasties 9–early 11
2040–1700 B.C.	Middle Kingdom	Dynasties 11–13
1700–1559 B.C.	Second Intermediate Period	Dynasties 14–17
1559–1085 B.C.	New Kingdom	Dynasties 18–20

*Most dates in Egyptian chronology are approximate.

FOR FURTHER READING

Fairfield, Helen N. *Everyday Life in Ancient Eygpt*. New York: G. P. Putnam's Sons, 1964,

Fairservis, Walter A., Jr. *Egypt, Gift of the Nile*. New York: The Macmillan Company, 1963.

Glubok, Shirley. *The Art of Egypt under the Pharaohs*. New York: The Macmillan Company, 1980.

Green, Roger Lancelyn. *Tales of Ancient Egypt*. New York, Henry Z. Walck, 1968.

Katan, Norma J. and Mintz, Barbara. *Hieroglyphs: The Writing of Ancient Egypt*. New York: Atheneum Publishers, 1981.

Macaulay, David. *Pyramid*. New York: Houghton Mifflin Company, 1975.

Pace, Mildred Mastin. *Wrapped for Eternity: The Story of the Egyptian Mummies*. New York: McGraw-Hill, 1974.

Payne, Elizabeth. *The Pharaohs of Ancient Egypt*. New York: Random House, 1964.

Price, Christine. *Made in Ancient Egypt*. New York: E.P. Dutton, 1970.

INDEX